The Heart of Mother

The Heart of Mother

By

George Campbell Hage
Ed. D., Ph. D., LPCS

One Spirit Press
Portland, Oregon

ISBN: 9781793943811

One Spirit Press
onespiritpress.com
onespiritpress@gmail.com

Table Of Contents

Acknowledgments

This short book grew out of the chapter, The Heart of Mom in Counseling. Beginning there, I recalled my experience with mothers and their sons over the years of my counseling career. Also, I was empowered to reenter my childhood and adolescent years with my mother. Being 65 at the time, I had already been counseling 20 years. But at this time, I realized the forming of my legacy, namely, the story originally given to me by my mother. Through each of these chapters, I recall her wisdom and insights transpiring through the lives of my mothers' relating to their children in the counseling relationship. Hence, I was empowered to effectively call youth clients to receive the wisdom of their mothers. The heart of mom is shown to be in "learning," "knowing," "the father," "community," "love," "faith," "of the child," "the senior," "virtue," "wisdom," "counseling," and "as the child." My prayer is that these pages will inspire all who read its pages including mothers, counselors, and educators.

I decided to publish these essays as chapters through the encouragement of my sister, Camille Anna Hage Thorne, MA. She has been a high school teacher over the years of English, French, and German. She took the time to read each one and order them according to their meaning. I wish to acknowledge her for her work and encouragement of these essays as chapters.

I also want to thank the publisher, Suzanne Deakins, Ph., D, for her love, guidance, and encouragement for this and my other writings. She offered the publication of this book as a surprise Christmas gift to me and my wife. In conjunction with her hard work, dedication, and self-sacrifice, she managed the publication of this and seven other books. She has also authored and many works over the years.

George Campbell Hage

Forward

Mother's Incomparable Value
Mother's worth exceeds value beyond compare.
Even precious beyond earthly comprehension is
she.
With understanding superseding that of others,
Her ableness astounds the mind's awareness.

Mother knows her child as no other can.
Not even her child knows as mother can.
Her child, was nearer beyond imagination,
Touched her heart within her bosom.

She, through the womb sensed,
Through every cell in sync with hers,
The wonder of the beating heart,
The message of fluttering motions
In sync with every sigh of every breath.

A union beyond compare,
Exceeding every earthly apprehension,
The soul of a child born in the womb
Through the heart of mother,
The very eye of her soul.

In mystery, mother sees a child unseen,
And receiving the child as hers.
Two persons now in sync,
Becoming flesh of flesh and bone of bone.
Being one,
A marriage beyond compare.

The Heart of Mother

"I will look after you and I will look after anybody you say needs to be looked after, any way you say. I am here. I brought my whole self to you. I am your mother."

Maya Angelou, Mom & Me & Mom

Mother The Heart of Learning

Mother becomes the heart of learning for her child. Mother is the first teacher. She by nature instills within her child the power of learning. How does this happen, one may ask? As both a counselor and educator over the years, I have experienced the reality and power of learning as a natural endowment in small children.

Children in preschool and early elementary school naturally love to learn. They see learning experiences as fun, and through the natural motivation of play, they are able to take on any learning experience. They feel no hesitance or fear no matter the task given to them by their teacher or parent.

Children as with all humankind, are endowed with spark and power of creativity. In reality, creativity is the very reflection of the image of God. That is, God, in the beginning created so states the Genesis 1 account, "On the very first day of being God creates being, beginning with the heavens and the earth."

Children receive that God-given spark of creativity through their mothers. As the womb of mother creates a new life, a child of creativity enters the world with renewing power. Through humankind over the centuries, we see children who have grown into the genius of creating through art, architecture, science, inventing, music, literature, and the like.

In reality, this way of learning of children is manifested in the inner person of children. This person or self, if you will, is the little child that is to remain in us and grow with us in the experience of living. Of course, mother is a vital part of the mystery of this growing and maturing child. Hence, learning complemented by mother must foster counseling and education that is conducive to the tender self of children. Such curriculum must roll with children and mother, ever stimulating and motivating their creative energies.

In all, curriculum centered on mother and child provides learning experiences related to varied subject matters while counseling involving mother assists teaching in personalizing the learning experience of knowledge geared to children. Together teaching and counseling mold the developing personality of the true and creative self in maturing and growing children.

In essence, the power of creative curriculum and counseling remains connected to the mothers of children. For this reason, the source of the true self and creative power of children exudes from the heart of mom. In bearing and birthing her child and while caressing her precious gift to her bosom, mom transmits God-like creative energy into the heart of the child.

From mother, the child acquires language, and with language comes every creative thought, concept, and emotion. Furthermore, the amazement of this is summed up in the uniqueness of creative personalities comprising every child. But, even exceeding this wonderful reality, and yet fundamental to its life, is the reality of love.

In fact, mother from the beginning of conception teaches her child to love through the love that she gives to this new and budding person. Essentially, mother, through loving, is teaching love while also fostering creative learning through play in her child. Furthermore, true creative learning involves the power of loving the objects and experience of learning. Hence, this natural endowment of children is due to the reality that mom has conveyed to them the power of love for all things. That is, no division exists between children and the objects of their experiential and creative learning.

In all, mother must never be left out of the equation of curriculum and counseling, of teaching and learning, as she provides the channel through which children may foster their true creative energies on into adulthood.

Mama was my greatest teacher, a teacher of compassion, love and fearlessness. If love is sweet as a flower, then my mother is that sweet flower of love.

Stevie Wonder

Mother the Heart of Knowing

From my mother's womb, I began to know. Her emotions, her impulses, the rhythm of her breath and beating heart moved upon me. These were my first sentients of being and knowing. Her awareness became mine. Her feelings and thoughts began to mold me. As the writer pens thoughts, feelings, and emotions upon a manuscript, I became my mother's manuscript.

Through mother, I began to know. Through initial sentients, I entered into feelings beyond my feeling, thoughts beyond my thought. I learned through intuiting. Such knowing was impressionable and real, yet beyond language rather than non-language.

In saying this of myself, I am saying for all in general that sentients begin our moldings into unique works of art. What appears general in the womb, in actuality, becomes specific for each of us. As the artist with canvas, paint, and brush, the sculptor with clay, Plaster of Paris, and mold, and the author with pen, ink, and manuscript, mother begins the impressionable idea of our person and being into portraiture and story.

As she watches over the ways of her household, she watches over the ways of her womb. She sets us off in the initial path of our life, so that later we will not lose the way. This path is etched and written into our heart and imprinted upon the lesions of our brain. It becomes wired into our neural pathways.

Mother forgets not the child of her womb and breasts. By divine spark, she intuitively remembers in the face of forgetting. She stands as a guard at the temple gate, minding whatever and whomever may enter. Her womb is her child's inner sanctum, her breasts, her outer sanctum, and her home, her outmost sanctum.

These three sacred spheres of wisdom, protect, nurture, counsel, teach, and guide her child. In all three areas, she forswears idleness. She is given only to wisdom. Her source for wisdom stems from the womb of her bosom relating with her child. This relationship from the onset fostered in love, protection, nurturing, and care spawns living wisdom undefinable.

For this reason, mother knows our comings in and goings out. Although apart from us, she is close to us. Whether near or far, she knows of our danger. Even with those with whom we associate, she knows whether they are for our good or our ill. Whether as an adult or a child, these principles remain true.

Take time, therefore, to look into your childhood, and, undoubtedly, you will remember at least one instance in which your mother, who was far away from you, in her own way made you aware as to what you were up to or what was going on with you. Also, as an adult, consider carefully your mother's advice regarding a relationship that you are forming. Understand her knowing of you more than you know yourself, for she conceived and birthed you from the womb. And in her knowing, she knows your friends. She reads their hearts through yours. In all of this and many other experiences, she is teaching you wisdom, for her heart is wisdom.

In the end, above all else, Mom, as a soldier clad in armor, stands against the odds for the sake of her home and children. She bears within herself the brave heart of the man, father, and husband.

Mother, the Heart of Father

Reflecting over my life, growing up, teaching, ministering, and counseling, the value of mother has led me to see her power working through the heart of husband and father. Although my dad was away at work and out of touch with us children much of the day, my mother would often chide us or assure us: "I am telling your daddy when he gets home!" Essentially, when we were good, demonstrating compliant behavior, we became happy with the sure expectation of being rewarded at least with acceptance and praise from our dad. On the other hand, if our behavior was "bad," namely, showing noncompliance, we felt the fear and anxiety of some kind of oncoming punishment whether verbal or otherwise.

Hence, we were often left wondering as to the manner of the reward or punishment. Yet mother knew that dad would come to her defense because of the bond of mutual love between them. Of course, the energy of this love most likely stemmed from the heart of mom mutually embracing dad's heart. Dad was impelled to work daily in order to provide sustenance and protection for mom and us children. At the same time, mom joined dad in this endeavor especially through assisting in his calling as provider. Furthermore, when dad was unable to totally meet that demand, mom was always present to fill that need.

As in the beginning, when God created Eve from the side of Adam, so she emerged forth as his help-meet. That is, she was Adam's compliment and fulfillment, so what dad is unable to complete, mom completes it. This, in fact, is evident even when dad is out of the picture.

Specifically, the basic family unit in the United States traditionally was made up of father, mother, and children. This family content provided the traditional picture of the family. At this point in time, though, we are experiencing a transition in family content and structure. This becomes very apparent with the absence of father and husband for varied reasons including death and divorce.

Furthermore, I have been experiencing usually that mom and often grandmother carry on the rearing and managing of their families. This manifests the power of the mothering instinct. That is, the heart of mom contains the power of dad. This is manifested through mom's undying love for her children and family. She provides, nurtures, protects, and manages. She often accomplishes this alone on a daily basis while continuing through the years of rearing her children into adulthood.

The genius of mom lies in her power to juggle many tasks and demands in order to meet her many responsibilities. Even when father is at home, she provides and cares for him. Mom's heart is all-encompassing. She actually demonstrates not only the heart of dad but also the heart of home. Traditionally, society has looked to dad for leadership in the home, but mom's heart provides the power of that leadership which also is all-encompassing.

Mom, in all, displays powers of standing firm in times of threats and struggles. She, through her heart of love, becomes the shield of faith standing against every enemy against her home and children. She remains a bulwark with husband and father, or in his absence, she maintains the same stance (Ephesians 5:10-18). I cannot help but think of the song sung by Helen Redding in 1974, "It's me and you against the world." In the end, above all else, Mom, as a soldier clad in armor, stands against the odds for the sake of her home and children. She bears within herself the brave heart of the man, father, and husband.

Where we love is home - home that our feet may leave, but not our hearts.

Oliver Wendell Holmes, Sr.

Mother, the Heart of Home and Community

In my service as a counselor and therapist, I have often found myself relating to either the mother or grandmother along with one or more children in a given family. The father was often absent from the family, usually due to tragic circumstances. Hence, the family structure was often comprised of the mother in the absence of the father or even the maternal grandmother in the absence of the mother and father. This most likely is true across the board of differing cultures and ethnicities. At the same time, I would often relate to significant others in the outer context of the family.

Of course, in counseling, my focus has usually been on the child of adolescent age who was often involved in school. Such a context provided significant others among friends, relatives, school staff, medical personnel, and even another therapist or counselor.

What we learn here is that the family, in reality, is not as a cell living alone. Rather it is connected with other cells of the outer context, including even the expansiveness of the greater community. We may liken such interrelatedness to the human body in which one cell connects with many, thereby, receiving its energies from the context of the community as well as from the cellular family unit itself. We further understand this family unit, along with its intrinsic energies, as the home.

In this light, we apply the concept, energies, as referring to the many vital aspects of life-giving properties of exchange not only within the family unit, but also from outside of the family unit, namely, the family macrocosm or community energized by many family units and homes.

In the family unit, mother or grandmother provides the heart, the source of life-giving energies of the home. Her energies reach through the children into the social context of the family. Through her, the children become nurtured in wisdom, which also includes the properties of beliefs and values. These, in turn, provide the base of knowledge from which her children will link with knowledge from schooling and relationships in the community.

Mother, being the heart becomes the nucleus of the cell. The cell along with the nucleus, contains many properties that give it organic life. Such life is evidenced in the interactions and behaviors of the children with one another yet centers on the mother.

From infancy, the mother nurtures her children in the knowledge of culture with its struggles and gains and losses, along with the awareness of specific gifts and talents endowed by nature and nature's God. These children learn their first words from their mother through embrace and caressing speech. They eventually become empowered to change these words into precepts and concepts.

Through mother, they grow into a nurtured self, forming an identity. Such a self is the very image of mom yet miraculously unique to each child. This is the natural self that gradually moves beyond the content of the home into the context around the home.

Reflectively, the single cell interacts with other cells that, in turn, interact with one another. They generate life-giving energies to one another, thereby, energizing the organic life of the community.

In essence, home is the community within the community. Each family unit together through the interactions of mom, father, and children molds the greater community. Their beliefs and values provide the cultural core and knowledge base of this community. Also, this dynamic of exchange of energies between home and context gives life to the greater community. In all, mother provides the heart of the home while, the home, in turn provides the heart of the community.

Even though the face of families is changing shape and becoming new in form, the heart and source of the family remains the same, namely, that of mom. I see this miracle manifesting itself beyond the intricacies of verbal language. As her son or daughter struggles in counseling, I cannot help but witness mom's understanding, tenderness, empathy, and struggles with her child's struggles. For in the case of her child, she manifests a unique empathy beyond common understanding. As she felt the heart of her child beat in her womb, she still feels that same heartbeat in union with hers. As she sensed her baby's emotions in every breath, she continues maintaining the harmony of two hearts, those of mother and child.

Love isn't created out of feelings, emotions, or saying I do. But is the container in which we grow and become intimate with all life.

From Sacred Intimacy

Mother, the Heart of Love

The first virtue learned by a person is that of love. Although divine, it is the most natural of virtues in that love is received beginning in the womb of mother. Already, the developing child is felt by mom through her heart and bosom. Through the impulses of her heart, she is committing to her child to the point of giving the essence of her life to the child.

Undoubtedly, that essence is love, for the child, like us, is conceived in love, the mutual affection and union of man and woman as father and mother. As the Spirit of God was breathed into Adam, molded from the clay of the earth, so God breathes into Adam again and again, husband and wife commingled as one person and being, and this person is given new life by the breath of God. This breath of love from the overshadowing of the Highest One upon the body of man and woman complements both into one whole being.

The one person united by love for the other and further complemented by the overshadowing love of the Divine receive the breath of the Spirit into the womb of mom. This mystery of conception and gestation unto birthing is beyond a thorough explanation of science, for its mystery rests with the wisdom of the One.

And even more so than the explanation of science, can I, as a male and the father of my child, understand. For, unlike my wife, I have not conceived and given birth to my daughter. I had watched her mother give birth, and I assisted in the birthing, but I could not even begin to experience my wife's experience. I could only guess and only ask God to give me the wisdom to understand this mystery. True apprehension of this wonder is left to the experience of my wife and to the experience and wisdom of God.

Yet, through her experience, God imparts the wisdom of creation to her. Thus, unlike me or anyone else, she alone knows her child. She truly understands and reads the seeming unspoken messages of the child. She alone knows the rhythmic beating of the heart, the rhythmic breathing of the child, the pulsating flow of blood, and her child's overall tonality and manner.

As with every movement in the womb, so mother continues to hear and feel her growing child. No matter how near or far, she continues to hear her child's voice and that soul's rhythm of breathing, sighing, and walking. At the same time, she feels and senses her child's presence, tonality, manner and rhythm of voice, breathing, sighing, stepping, and behavior.

In this light I can say to the youth whom I teach and counsel: "Your mother knows you more than you know yourself." She knows where you are at all times and in all places whether she is near or far from you. She alone knows your voice as you know hers. She alone knows your scent and your presence even when you are not present. And whether you are far from her or near to her, she knows your joys and your woes. She knows of your danger and your safety."

This is true because she first loved you and continues to nurture you in her love. She loved you before you were conceived, and her love continues with you through eternity. From her love you experienced the first spark of life engendered by her love. And in your gestation, birthing, maturation, and development you learned her love because you grew in it. Such love is the chief virtue and power of life itself. The love you now have and give is your mother's love.

I remember my mother's prayers and they have always followed me. They have clung to me all my life.

Abraham Lincoln

Mother, the Heart of Prayer and Faith

In my mother, I first experienced prayer. As a young child, I remember walking in the ally next to my house, talking with God. Looking back, I wondered why I found myself doing that. Probably, I was 7 or 8 at the time. The sun was out and the weather that day was mild. The alley was made of bricks most likely laid during the Great Depression. Nevertheless, I remained fascinated by the shapes and indentures of the bricks as I walked alone.

I remember my mother from time to time talking to me about God: how he watched me and cared for me. She affirmed in me that although unseen he remained present with me. So, I found myself unafraid being alone, and often found myself lavishing in my aloneness with my teddy bear and toys. Walking also became a past-time for me. In walking, I gazed not only at the brick alleys and streets, but at the clouds and the sky along with the birds flying above.

I found myself also fascinated by the late afternoons as they moved into the evenings at dusk. I listened to the locusts and was moved by the early appearance of sparse fireflies. Then I would be moved to talk to God and sing a song.

My world was one of security because of the assurance of mother's ever-presence. This ever- presence was affirmed in the stories that she often told me about Jesus, God, and my guardian angel. In her assurance of the divine presence with me, she, in reality, was guaranteeing her presence with me.

Through such experiences, our mothers taught us the power and value of prayer and faith. We learned self-assurance, safety, and trust. We learned to look beyond ourselves for answers to questions as well as solutions to problems. We learned to build friendships and relationships based upon mother's example of trust and assurance.

Our mothers taught us how to feel safe when alone. They gave us our sense of confidence and self-esteem. They guided us in our relationships. Our mothers exercised wisdom and insight in knowing whether or not a new relationship would work toward our betterment. From experiences, we learned the insight and skillfulness of developing friends and relationships.

In all, our mothers gave us the sense of belonging. Through faith and prayer, they taught us of being at home in life. By imparting the sense of faith in the divine presence, we became empowered to find our place with self and others in the world.

In recalling those moments with our mothers, especially visions of little things from the past, we learned through years of struggles that our mothers gave us hope. In their living examples and stories of love, she taught us faith and prayer through which comes hope.

Mother's love is peace. It need not be acquired, it
need not be deserved.

Erich Fromm

Mother, the heart of Her Child

Growing up, you may learn that mom became the substance of your heart. I am sure that as you ponder your childhood and experiences and those of moving into adolescence and adulthood, you may certainly begin to see the power of this reality.

Perhaps you may recall your mom when she held you, carried you, and cuddled you. She would tell you that she loved you. She would speak to you in language only you could understand. Others would call this baby talk, but you surely did not think so. Rather, this was mom speaking with you in her own special language just for you.

How must mom have felt as she bore you in her womb? Can you even begin to perceive that she in gestation experienced the fullness of your developing life? In one sense you were as the caterpillar in a cocoon or a nucleus in an egg. You were totally unaware of your maturation unto blossoming as the butterfly or the bird. However, mother thoroughly knew you from conception through gestation unto birth, and from birthing, unto full development and maturation.

She experienced your very heart beats and life rhythms. She experienced the multiplication of your cells from one to the many translating in the newness of you. Then from birthing on to blossoming as the butterfly or the bird, she sees and feels the development of every cell unto the fullness of adulthood.

Because of your conception and gestation within her being, she experienced every message of your heart and life. Her heart and life thusly are at one with yours. For this reason, she knows you more than your father, your grandparents, and even more than you know yourself. In all, no one knows us as does mother.

In reality, mother is your guide and your light. She is your sure counselor and advocate. Only she may bear witness to the uniqueness of your person and being. As with the butterfly, she knows every tone and texture substantiating your personality. As the feathers and wings of the bird, she knows of your ability and strength enough to walk, run, and fly and she knows the strength and power of your senses to know where to fly.

Can you even begin to imagine or much less comprehend the breadth and depth of mom's knowledge? She does not merely apprehend the outer beauty of the Zebra Swallowtail butterfly or that of the Mandarin Duck. Rather mom has lived inside of your conception, gestation, and birthing. Although you were inside of mom's womb and being, she enveloped you from within and without.

Hence, your body is her body. Your mind is her mind, and your personality is her personality. In all, your life is her life, your being is her being, and your heart is her heart. Such is the mystery of mother.

LOVE is not about how many days, months or years you've been together. LOVE is about how much you love each other EVERYDAY.

Mother, the Heart of the Senior

Often times, I find myself reflecting back on my youth and childhood. Interestingly, these reflections often are unintentional. They seem to fly by, and thus they impress me before I totally realize them. Within, these visions at times will manifest my mother. She appears in many ways and contexts.

Mother becomes manifest during her caresses, hugs, and kisses. Holding me in her arms and talking to me. At times in "baby talk" and at other times telling me stories. She tells me she loves me, and from the depths of her heart she speaks words conveying feelings of beauty and self-worth to me.

I recall the many hours that mother spent with me in my elementary school years teaching me. She saw my talents in art and music and nurtured them. She drew and painted by my side. She felt deeply for me as I had a difficult time talking until I spoke my first word, *train*. I was close to 5 years at that time.

Thus, mother spent much time teaching me to read and speak. She paid money so that I would under-go private speech and drama lessons. I even remem-

ber having to memorize many poems. I vividly remember nervously delivering the Halloween poem
"Brooms" in a recital. I also recall my experience
with the drama, "The Gingham Dog and the Calico
Cat." Furthermore, I vividly recall taking my role as
the Calico Cat so literally that I deeply scratched my
peer, a girl, playing the Gingham Dog. Not only did
my speech teacher chide me for this, but my mother
also joined in with her.

I remember this greatly distressing and embarrass-
ing me. I remember the guilt, shame, and remorse
that I felt, especially coming from my mother. Within
myself, I was just trying to be the cat, thinking that
I would be pleasing to others, but instead, I strongly
felt my displeasure from mother and the teacher, and
making it worse, the girl's mother was upset with me
as well.

As, you may see, mother was the powerhouse in
my life. She grounded me in the sensitivity to right
and to wrong and to fantasy and reality. Most of all,
I learned the wrongness of hurting others even if
it was in play and fantasy. But over the years, she
continued to ground me in my studies and began to
teach me music and saw to my music lessons formal-
ly. She was studying the piano and voice. She played
very well, and displayed a pleasant mezzo soprano
voice. I heard her day after day playing and singing
the scales.

Through junior high and high school, piano became my post of authority at school and became my past time at home. Being engrossed in playing composers such as Chopin, Beethoven, and Bach, gave me comfort through my academic struggles. Nevertheless, my mother continued to work with me academically, artistically, and musically. At nights when my dad came home from work, he would sit and listen to me play. In fact, my father displayed a lyric tenor voice and could play the piano very well. He would often play parts of Rachmaninoff's Prelude in C Sharp Minor.

I was strongly encouraged to move on in time studying music through high school and college, and later in graduate school I branched off into philosophies of education, anthropology, and religion.

Now that I am in my senior years, I realize that my mom guided the formation of my legacy with my father joining her at the helm. Without mother, we seniors would not have a story to leave with our children and grandchildren. She helped us to form our first words and symbols. She gave us our first thoughts and feelings and their relationships to these words and symbols. She even initiated our belief and value systems and ultimately our behaviors.

In most two parent families, dad later joins in with mom in teaching, encouraging, and affirming us in the formation of our talents and interests. They spend much time in shaping the foundations of our story so that in growing older the story becomes a fully branched and blossoming tree.

In all, mom not only is the heart of a child, but she demonstrates the heart of dad. In fact, mom's heart is a big heart with lots of room for the whole of her family. As her heart provides the seed of our story, so it provides the wisdom of the senior.

George Campbell Hage

All good virtues and goodness itself will gradually find their true home in the heart in which love
dwells, and all other qualities will wither and die.

Ritu Ghatourey

Mother, The Heart of Virtue

If you are seeking virtue, return to the love of your mother. In reality, love yields every virtue, so you must strive to recapture that love. Love is the primary fount of all natural and spiritual virtues, and I submit that all virtues including the natural are also spiritual. There is no true distinction between the good of nature and the Spirit of being.

We have said in another piece, that love stems from the heart of mom for her child. She first loved her child at conception and continued mothering through gestation and beyond birthing. She held her child upon her bosom and nursed it with her breasts. Her child was in and grew next to her heart.

Recall the love that you experienced from your mother's womb to growing up at home. Remember her closeness to you even when you believed you were far from her. Remember her long suffering through your struggles from the slightest bruise on your knee to mishaps at school and feelings of rejection and failure. In remembering with prayer, you will acquire patience, for in giving the same love of your mother to others, you will find greater ease for patience and long suffering through your relationships and trials.

From patience with love, you will find gentleness and kindness. Others will welcome you as friendly and warm. Think of those moments of love and affection with tenderness that you spent with your mother, and you will certainly realize this in your relations with others.

In reality, mother's heart is the fount of every virtue because she is a wellspring of love. Consider the beautiful words of St. Paul: "Love is patient, love is kind, it does not envy, it does not boast, it is not proud. It does not dishonor others. It is not self-seeking, it is not easily angered, it keeps no record of wrongs. Love does not delight in evil but rejoices with the truth. Love always protects, always trusts, always hopes, always perseveres" (1 Corinthians 13:4-7 NIV).

All virtue is strongly suggested in these words. In all, the power to love yields patience, forgiveness, humility, meekness, the ability to joy in other's lives and successes, and to walk gratefully for even the little things that come your way. Also, love impels you to show honor and respect for others. Love yields faithfulness in relationships while free from adulteration.

Looking to your mother, you may capture the many instances of her willingness to sacrifice her own needs and desires in order to grant yours. The steadfastness and fidelity of your mother's love was undoubtedly demonstrated in her willingness to provide for your needs and desires first with her hard-earned money before spending anything on herself. She reached out to you on your birthday, on holidays, and other special occasions. She provided for your school needs, your clothing needs, and your needs for food and medical care. She struggled to provide a safe and secure and nurturing home so that you would thrive.

These virtues are many and extremely powerful and healing. Especially when you recall, ponder, and meditate on them while applying them to your life. Truly, this was your mother's legacy to you. She already etched these into your heart and mind so that you may reach out to your children and others with her profound love.

Where there is charity and wisdom, there is neither fear nor ignorance.

Francis of Assisi

Mother, The Heart of Wisdom

Now that I am in my senior years, I have come to realize that my mother knew the thoughts of my heart. I remember one particular day when I was a boy, she was in one room at one end of our home on the upper floor while I was in another room on the lower floor at the opposite end of our home. She was running the sewing machine, and as I began pondering in my heart to do wrong, she yelled, calling me by my nickname, "Cam! Cut that out!

Since that day, I had forgotten that experience until my 28th year as a counselor of young boys and my memory of this incident was aroused. While counseling with a 14-year old boy and his mother, his natural resistance to her sound advice enlivened that clairvoyant wisdom of my mother. During those moments, "I was able to encourage him through narrative to receive the meaningfulness of his mother's advice."

I had emphasized to him: "Your mother knows you better than you know yourself. She knows your very heart beats as she bore you in her womb. You rested in her bosom, being the nearest to her heart. Hence, when you learn your heart as she knows yours, then you will know her heart, and there you will find wisdom."

Wisdom, unlike the knowledge we acquire from books and in school, supercedes these. In the ancient Greek understanding, wisdom was named as such in the feminine gender, Sophia. Mother by her very nature translates knowledge into wisdom. She is empowered with a heart that intuits hidden meaning by what most of us define as concrete and real. Such human knowledge is often frozen into bits and chunks and defined by arbitrary systems of logic. Yet mom's wisdom lives beyond such human understanding.

Mom's wisdom flows from the bosom of her heart. In those undefined moments of time, she supernaturally listens and responds with words that directly feed the heart. Within brackets of time, she edifies the heart of the other with meaningful insight and hope. Her words arouse joy in the other, especially in the heart of her beloved child.

For years, I have heard her speak to her child, beginning with hearing my mother's voice calling out to me. Yes, even when she calls your name, she is speaking with you and building you up with insight and hope. Her voice, as you listen, empowers you with guidance to listen to your own heart and even to the hearts of others.

Once you receive her wisdom, you become transfigured through the union of your mind and heart. Thoughts and emotions remain no longer apart and in conflict. Rather emotions become thought laden and thoughts emotion laden, keeping restless passions at bay. Wisdom begins to wholly embrace you. Depression and anxiety become muted as we touch the golden mean.

Such balance of even temperateness and self-control proceeds from the heart of mom. This is her natural yet supernal gift to us. Imparted to us as children and even adults by her voice, she constantly woos us and guides us with wisdom.

This is true even beyond the grave. I cannot help but recall the last time I heard my mother's call to me. She had passed away in 2000. As a minister, I read from the psalms at her funeral but, another minister officiated. I did not shed a tear but remained in solemn reverence as if frozen. Yet two days later, having awakened from sleep, I suddenly heard her voice beside my bed call out to me gently, "Cam!" Unable to contain my emotions, I wept tearfully and profusely.

At that time, I was awakened to renewed moments of wisdom. My mother's heart had touched mine and mine hers. In bracketed moments of time, I had received her impartation of wisdom, an understanding beyond words and uncontainable joy.

I've had many mentors, but the one that has the most impact was my mother.

Ursula Burns

The Heart of Mother in Counseling

The family in traditional society has been comprised of a husband, wife, and child or children. Mom and wife provide the heart of the father and husband, and children provide the heart of the mother. In today's more heterogeneous societies, this mix may vary due to adoptions, foster care, and marriage and non-marital bonds that emerge from homosexual and transgender relationships.

But over the last 28 years of counseling my interactions have been primarily with the mother and her children. At times the father of the child was involved but most of the time he was not. Hence, the primary family core was mother and child.

Mothers demonstrate by nature heart and passion for their child. Mother also conveys heart and passion for either her husband or the father of her child. Mother's heart in reality conveys the life and bond of the family.

Mother bore her child in her womb for nine months, and in birthing, felt great pain emerging from her being and that of her child. In conceiving and carrying her child, she experienced the baby's growth, movements, and messages from the forming heart of the child to her heart.

In counseling with her and her child, I have learned that mom knows her child even more than the child knows him-or herself. No matter the age of the child, whether 7 or 17, she knows the heart and mind of her child. Interestingly, I am very fond of the way African American mothers refer to their sons and daughters even if 17 or older as baby.

The power of that metaphor conveys nurturing love and caring, the depth of understanding the message of the child, and the unique and intricate personality of the child. Regarding the first two ideas, mom holds her child next to her heart and much of the time nourishes his or her very being from her breasts. Through her breasts flow not only physical nourishment but also the intimate exchange of edifying messages of spirit and mind. In mom's embrace, the art of her child's personality is shaped.

In essence, the personality of the child is a work of art first in scripted by mom. As unique and complete as the different fingerprints and brain maps of different people, so is her child's personality. She is the artist and her child the work of art. As the artist knows his work, she alone knows hers.

This dawned on me, much later in my life, despite my years of work with mom's children and families--this even despite all of my schooling and education. Such wisdom I believe comes not merely from books and even interactive experience. Rather, it comes from the heart.

As a counselor, I have developed and am still developing not only a truly professional love for my child clients but I also see myself cultivating a heart for my maternal clients. As a counselor, I see the high value of letting mother guide me in working with her child. In this way, I affirm her wisdom, and touch the heart of her child. In all, I see the wisdom in valuing the heart of mother specifically and that of women in general.

We are born of love; Love is our mother.

Rumi

The Heart of Mother, Her Child

Mother knows her child. Mother bore her child in her bosom, which is truly in union with her heart. That is, heart and bosom live within her breast giving the essence of life to her child. Following conception, her child grows and develops according to the rhythm of her being. Every beat of her heart synergizes with while energizing every beat of her child's heart.

Mother's rhythm of being sets the rhythm of being in her child. Every cell of her being receives and conveys every electrical impulse of her child. Her mind gives life to her child's mind as conveyed from her heart to the child's heart. At the time of conception and gestational maturity, Mom's mind and heart become synergized with the natural unity of her child's heart and mind.

Every cell of mom becomes every cell of her child. In their synergy, they are in essence sameness, but in form yet unique. Hence, within the womb cells are unfolding into primal identity and person. Also, we must not discount Dad's cells as being a vital part of the equation of primal person and identity. Yet, in reality, the heart and mind of mom even becomes the guiding impetus of Dad's identity giving form and essence to the child's total being and person.

Inwardly and outwardly, the child's traits of being manifest themselves from the living and breathing embryo to fetus and then infant at the close of gestation. Mother, herself, experiences the rhythmic pangs of birthing, which were implicitly emanating since conception. Like the earth, herself, who appears quiet outwardly, but yet pangs grow stealthily from her heart gradually into a state of frightening and woeful eruption. For as mother, she bears within herself the joys and sorrows of life emerging in terms of flora and fauna.

Mother's heart conveys the rhythms of cosmos in rhythms emanating from her heart and mind to the total being of her child. Thus, mother knows instinctively the undefined essence of cosmic life which is breathed through her to her child. Intrinsically, mother receives the wisdom of life's mind beyond human understanding. Yet due to this wisdom, she understands the heart, mind, and thereby, the total being of her child.

She alone has experienced conception, gestation, and birthing. She alone knows the joy amidst the sadness of trauma and pangs. She alone touches her child's essence and perceives the rhythm of its message. She breathes with her child, feels with her child, and moves with her child. She even listens to her child voice from within and even understands its message beyond the womb.

Such is the wonder and marvel of mother. So strong is her love that it gives life and being to her child. In conception, gestation, and birthing, her love yields patience and long-suffering. Her love yields fortitude, understanding, and selflessness. It yields knowing beyond knowing, for such love knows mystery--knowing emerging from the mystery of her child.

Colophon

Titles in Apple Chancery
Text in Times New Roman

Apple Chancery by Kris Holmes, commissioned by Apple in 1993. Holmes had been taught calligraphy at Reed College, by the same tutors as Steve Jobs (though not at the same time). The font's goal was to include complex alternates to somewhat mimic the verve of Renaissance scribes.

Times New Roman gets its name from the Times of London, the British newspaper. In 1929, the Times hired typographer Stanley Morison to create a new text font. Morison led the project, supervising Victor Lardent, an advertising artist for the Times, who drew the letter forms.

55

Mother is the name for God in the lips and hearts of little children.

William Makepeace Thackeray

Fini